On the Bathroom Floor Looking Up

Encouragement for when you think you are down for the count!

On the Bathroom Floor Looking Up

Encouragement for when you think you are down for the count!

Linda Rollins

Scripture quotations are taken from KJV, the King James Version of the Bible.
Scripture quotations are taken from NKJV, the New King James Version, Copyright 1982 by Thomas Nelson. Used by permission. All rights reserved.
Scripture quotations are taken from NLT, the New Living Translation copyright 1996, 2004, 2007. Used by permission of Tyndale House Publishers Inc., Wheaton, IL 60189 All rights reserved.
Scripture quotations are taken from NIV, the Holy Bible, New International Version, copyright 1973, 1978, 1984, 2011 by Biblica Inc. Used by permission, all rights reserved worldwide.
Scripture quotations are taken from TPT, The Passion Translation, Copyright 2017, 2018, 2020 by Passion & Fire Ministries, Inc. Used by permission. All rights reserved. The PassionTranslation.com
Scripture quotations are taken from ESV, the English Standard Version Bible, copyright 2001, 2012 by Crossway, a publishing ministry of Good News Publishers. All right reserved.

On The Bathroom Floor Looking Up

ISBN 979-8-36608-243-3

Copyright 2023 by Linda Rollins
All Rights Reserved

Contact Information
Linda Rollins
www.buckeyenative78@gmail.com
Facebook Linda Rollins
Instagram Buckeyekid78

DEDICATION

I'm thankful to God for all the lessons I've learned, and the growth from all the experiences in life I've had. All my praise goes to Jesus for shaping me into the woman I am today, and for His love, mercy, and grace. I stand in awe of Him as His perfect plan for me continues to unfold.

I'm thankful for my husband, Richard, who has encouraged me to write down my life experiences, so many of which he has shared with me. Many times, I don't know how I would have survived without his love, help and care for me.

I want to thank my children Scott and Dawn Marie, family and friends, who have shared in the ups and downs, blessings, and hard times. I could not have gotten through life without you. Your love and prayers have been my constant support.

A special thank you to Minister Lynda Puff, my mentor and friend, who has always been my role model. Your teachings inspire me, and your perseverance through tough times speaks volumes of encouragement!

Special thanks to Pastor Cindy Carpenter for your encouragement and guidance in this process.

Thanks to Dawn Marie Brown for reviewing and pulling all this together in a cohesive manner; your help has been invaluable.

CONTENTS

Introduction 6

Down for the Count 7

Nearly Drowning 13

Falling in the Bathroom 16

The Grocery Store Episode 19

Persevering 22

The Diagnosis 28

Tranquility 31

Expressions of His Love 34

Confronting Evil 37

Suffering 43

Lessons Learned 50

Choosing Him 54

Salvation Prayer 55

Introduction

Have you ever felt as though life was spiraling out of control, and you didn't have any answers as to why? I would have episodes of passing out, episodes that ended with me lying on the bathroom floor looking up; bloodied, bruised, shaken, and sometimes left with concussions, looking for answers that no doctor could give….

If you are going through tough times, I want to encourage you that God has not forgotten you. He is right there with you every step of the way. Don't give up! Look up!

DOWN FOR THE COUNT!

Have compassion on me, Lord, for I am weak. Heal me, Lord, for my bones are in agony. I am sick at heart. How long, O Lord, until you restore me?
Psalm 6:2-4 NLT

"Linda, wake up," my dad said, as he answered the knock on the door. I lay napping on the sofa in our family room. "Mary is here to see you."

I got up and walked into the kitchen to greet my friend, but I never made it. What happened next would happen too many times to mention throughout my life, and the mystery of it would not be solved for many years. I passed out about halfway through the kitchen falling hard on the linoleum floor and pulling down our parakeet, Tippy, along with his cage. Tippy was okay, but birdseed and feathers went everywhere! My parents and my friend Mary were in shock. Mary had become a part of this scene by simply stopping by to return the album I had loaned her, The Doors. That album was a big selling hit in the 1960s. She and I thought there was no one quite like Jim Morrison of The Doors. We exchanged albums regularly throughout high school.

I remember that as I regained consciousness, my father was saying over and over, "Lindy, don't die! Please don't die!" (Lindy was his nickname for me growing up.) No one knew what had happened, and we wouldn't for another forty years. This was my earliest recollection of passing out. I was eighteen years old, working and going to college full-time. I often was very tired, and my parents would ask me, "Is this too much for you to do?" I didn't think it was, I was eighteen and had my whole life ahead of me. At that age, I thought more about the here and now as opposed to my future. I learned, however, my future would be greatly impacted by these mysterious "falling down" spells.

I grew up in a rural area of northeastern Ohio in a small town of about four hundred people. I was the younger of two daughters. My mom was a stay-at-home mom. My dad worked at a steel mill in western Pennsylvania about twenty miles away. It was a wonderful childhood for the most part. We lived just down the road from my maternal grandparents and their farm. Two sets of aunts, uncles, and cousins also lived within walking distance. Summers were spent outdoors, often in the backyard, playing with cousins and neighbors. I remember one summer night when I was eight or nine years old, my sister and I were in our front yard catching lightning bugs. We imprisoned them in a jar with air holes poked in the lid. (We always hoped they'd live, but most didn't survive even overnight.) It was a moonless, dark summer night with only the front porch light shining out a few feet. There were no streetlights to brighten things up as there are in the city.

We were at the side of our house, near a thicket of bushes where the lightning bugs congregated. My mom called us to come in so my sister went in first to take her bath. By this time the grass in the front yard was damp with evening dew, and when mom called me to come, I ran as fast as I could toward the house. My foot slipped on the damp grass sending me reeling headlong into the corner of the front porch. Cement is an unforgiving element! This accident left a huge, goose egg-sized bump on the front left side of my forehead. I remember being stunned, dizzy, nauseous, and hurting badly. My eyes began to water. I tried not to cry; I knew I'd be in trouble for not going inside when mom had first called. The goose egg was not something I could hide! When mom saw the bump, she immediately put ice on it to reduce the swelling. By the next morning, it was black and blue and still very much a huge lump. Over the next few days, thankfully, the swelling went down. My bangs hid the swelling which began turning shades of blue, purple, and yellow.

Years later, I found out this innocent accident *could* have been a cause of the electrical shorts and miscommunication that happen when my brain sends messages to my heart. A neurologist I would see in 2006 felt my problem was in the left frontal lobe of my brain, the very area I had hit on that corner of our concrete porch as a kid. Brain trauma can happen in any number of ways, but I think that hunting for lightning bugs and sliding into our porch corner was a unique way of *possibly* causing it! This incident preceded the episodes of fainting that went on for many years in my life. I remember so many, many times being on the bathroom floor, looking up and wondering what was going on! Dazed and confused! Even at that young age of eight or nine, whether I knew it or not, God had his hand on me. When I think about my life and the things that have happened to me, I know without a doubt that He has been there all along. I was often too preoccupied with myself or the problems at hand to acknowledge God. Thank heavens I realized before it was too late that He loves me! He has always loved me and He will never stop loving me! Just as He tells me in Jeremiah 31:3 "…. I have loved you with an everlasting love; therefore, I have continued my faithfulness to you."

NEARLY DROWNING

Heal me, oh Lord and I shall be healed; save me, and I shall be saved, for thou are my praise.
Jeremiah 17:14 NKJV

Once at a swim park in Hubbard, Ohio, I nearly drowned. It was the beginning of summer vacation and my dad had taken me to the swim park with a few friends. This was a treat since I typically wouldn't see my friends until school began again in the fall. Living in the country and having only one car made it difficult to spend time with any of my school chums during the summer.

The day was full of expectancy for lots of fun and swimming. The only trouble was that all my friends could swim, and I could only "doggie paddle"— and I wasn't very good at that! My friends headed to a large slide in the deep end of the water, and I followed them. As I climbed the ladder to the top, I knew I should have turned around and gotten down, but my pride wouldn't let me. I zoomed down the slide, went under the water, and immediately panicked – I couldn't touch the bottom! I remember putting my arm up out of the water hoping someone would grab my hand and rescue me… No one did. I was in a panic!

As I continued to struggle, I suddenly felt a great peace come over me, and I saw a vision of shining buildings sitting atop a hill. They glistened and shone white with gold. It was a sight I will never forget. Peace continued to flood into me, even as I took in more water and put my hand up another time. Suddenly, one of my friends grabbed my hand. She pulled me up out of the deep end. I've wondered since that time where the lifeguard was as I flailed around in the water. My dad was anxiously waiting for me on the side of the pool. I remember lying there spitting out water, so thankful someone had grabbed my hand! God bless my little girlfriend; I don't even remember which one pulled me up to safety!

That vision and the peace that accompanied it have stayed with me all of my life. I know that God had His eye on me and rescued me that day. It's one of those memories that never fade and I truly believe it was a glimpse of heaven!

It was years later that under God's watchful eyes, I did eventually learn to swim!

FALLING IN THE BATHROOM

My brethren, count it all joy when you fall into various trials, knowing that the testing of your faith produces patience.
James 1:2-3 NKJV

Fast forward a few years from my near-drowning experience, I was married and expecting our first child. The passing-out spells returned, and my doctor told me to take it easy. One day I was in the bathroom, feeling weak and clammy, and I knew I was going to pass out. As I went down, I grabbed the curtains on the window and pulled them with me. My head landed on the bathroom scale. When I came to, I realized my head hurt and was throbbing after hitting the scale dead on. From that point forward, the scale always registered ten pounds. It never went back to zero. That always made me laugh in the midst of these spells!

I passed out a lot during my pregnancy, but then after the birth of our baby boy, Scott, the spells seemed to disappear. This was the pattern that would continue for many years: seasons of episodes, followed by long periods of few or none.

I think this pattern gave me a false sense of being okay when I wasn't. Various doctors diagnosed me with abdominal migraines, panic attacks, low blood sugar, and low blood pressure, but no one could solve the mystery. A few years went by, and our second blessing, a baby girl named Dawn Marie, was born. I began experiencing an increase in the spells. It was more of the same diagnosis and advice from doctors, "Don't stand up too fast because you have low blood pressure." (I'd get dizzy and lightheaded.) After years of hearing this, I just learned to deal with it and not worry about it. During this time, with God's help, I was able to raise the kids, work full-time, and unfortunately, go through a divorce. I kept doing what I knew I had to do, one step at a time and one day at a time.

His mercy and faithfulness to me were new every morning just as Lamentations 3:22-23 says.

THE GROCERY STORE EPISODE

Come to me, all who labor and are heavy laden, and I will give you rest.
Mathew 11:28 ESV

As the years ticked on my son married and moved out, while my teenage daughter was still living at home with me. I began to have more fainting spells as I entered my forties, and many things seemed to trigger these spells. Exercise, changes in temperature, and eating too much sugar could all cause me to start sweating, feel nauseous, head to the bathroom. There I would pass out. Once, my daughter and I ate some yummy Dunkin Donuts, and in no time at all, I had a nasty reaction. My clothes got soaked from sweat, and all the other symptoms followed. To try and get cool during these spells I lay on the tile floor peeling off my clothes. Such a sight! Only time seemed to help the symptoms fade and they left my body exhausted. By this time, I was working two or three jobs to keep things afloat financially, and that took its toll on me. I worked a full-time job Monday through Friday, 7 a.m. to 3 p.m., cleaned offices in the evening four times a week until 10 p.m., as well as transcribing dictation for a doctor on the weekends.

One Friday evening, my daughter and I went grocery shopping. As we shopped, I had an episode. I knew I had to sit down, so I cleared out a bottom shelf in the magazine aisle. I sat with my head between my legs to hopefully prevent myself from passing out. My daughter was embarrassed that I did this, as other shoppers were staring at me as they passed by. I tried to remain calm and just push through this unpleasant episode.

After thirty minutes of sitting on the magazine shelving, I felt well enough to finish our shopping, weak and sweaty, and go home. Although I wasn't aware of it, God's grace was sufficient for me even then.

He saw me that day before eternity and all the other times I was sick and passed out: while shopping, while stepping out of a jacuzzi, while cross-country skiing, while at my desk at work, while cooking, while eating, while on a date, while at the beach, while walking to name a few.

Like the song says, "His eye is on the sparrow, and I know He watches me….." I was the sparrow on those days and His gaze was fixed on me.

PERSEVERING

Brothers, I do not consider that I have made it my own. But there is one thing I do: Forgetting the things that are behind and straining toward the things that are ahead.
Philippians 3:13 ESV

In my forties and fifties, the passing out spells got worse and more frequent, some even required an ambulance ride to the ER! One evening, I had a friend over to watch a movie. As we ate popcorn and drank sodas, I got up to change the channel on the TV because it didn't have a remote. Suddenly, I passed out cold. My friend was trying to revive me when I woke up. He was so unnerved seeing me pass out from what seemed like nothing that he decided to go home and let me rest. I felt better, or so I thought….I got up to walk him out and passed out again! Well, this was too much for him. He got me comfy on the sofa and left. I scared him away!

Years passed, and I married again. This time to a wonderful man who enjoys hiking and the outdoors. We started hiking Camelback Mountain, in Arizona, every weekend. We were training for a hike to the Havasupai Indian Reservation, at the southwest corner of the Grand Canyon, to see the beautiful waterfalls there. It would be a ten-mile hike in and out; we would be camping there for a few days. We had to carry in and out all we needed including a tent, food, clothes, any supplies, and trash. On the hike in I began to get sick. We had to stop a few times to alleviate the symptoms I was having, but it wasn't enough. I began sweating, getting dizzy and nauseous…..another spell! I had to sit and rest so often that it delayed our descent into the canyon by an hour or two. Luckily, once we got there, I was okay and didn't have any more symptoms even on the hike back out. After that, we continued hiking frequently on Camelback Mountain. I would tell my husband and his friend, Dan, who often accompanied us, to go on ahead and I'd catch up. I was dizzy and nauseous, but I just wouldn't give in to it. I look back on how foolish that was. To climb a mountain while being dizzy is not using wisdom!

At this time, I had been working at a veterinary hospital doing HR and payroll for several years. I loved it! There wasn't a better place for an animal lover to be employed. I met so many wonderful people during the thirteen years I worked there. One day, my boss and I were running errands and buying items for gift bags we were assembling for Employee Appreciation Day. We stopped at Starbucks to get coffee, and a snack and then proceeded to a Bath & Body Works store. It was the holiday season so there were lots of colorful holiday displays inside the store. Candles, creams, lotions, body sprays, soaps, and more were strategically placed among all the glitter and holiday sparkle lining the shelves. As my boss and I looked around inside, Christmas music was playing and I started not feeling well. I leaned up against a small sink inside the store, while my friend purchased items for the gift bags. She looked back at me, and she could tell I didn't feel well. Then before I knew what happened, I passed out cold in the store. I woke up with people all around me, and paramedics were there to check me out. They took my vitals and advised me to go to the hospital, but I foolishly declined believing I was okay. They told me to see my doctor; they left and I went back to work as though all was well with me.

From that point on, things seemed to get worse. I started having more spells at work and home. I was even sent to a neurologist who checked me for seizures. He prescribed a seizure medication which caused mental fog, not good when I was responsible for doing payroll! I couldn't drive while on the medication so my husband,

Richard, became my chauffeur, driving me to work and everywhere else I needed to go.

One weekend our church had a community picnic/outreach at a local park. My husband and I were there helping. We took a break and went to donate blood at the bloodmobile that was visiting the park that day. We walked back across the grass to the picnic area, we realized how hot it was, and I decided to get a snow cone from the stand our church had set up. I reached out for the lime flavor cone I'd ordered; suddenly I felt weak, a grayness seemed to envelop me, and I knew I was going to pass out. I turned and faintly called for my husband, but I ended up passing out on the concrete sidewalk and knocking the back of my head a good one! The ambulance took me to the hospital where doctors checked me out and released me with a concussion to monitor at home. They advised me to see not only a neurologist, which I was already doing but a cardiologist, too. I never thought there was anything wrong with my heart, but the ER doctor thought it was worth getting a cardiology examination.

During these years I persevered through medical challenges that could have killed me. I survived regardless of my ignorance and at times bad judgments. I praise God that He never left my side and He saw me through it all! As a quote by Tim Keller, a pastor, and author says, "You don't realize God is all you need until God is all you have."

THE DIAGNOSIS

And be sure of this: I am with you always, even to the end of the age. Mathew 28:20b NLT

I immediately made an appointment with a cardiologist hoping to finally get answers to the cause of these spells. The doctor specialized in electrical issues, which was what the ER doctor thought my problem might be. The cardiologist examined me. I told him what had been happening all my life. He looked at me and said he knew *exactly* what the problem was: cardio-neurogenic syncope, a miscommunication between the brain, heart, and vagus nerve. The vagus nerve, also known as the vagal nerves, are the main nerves of your parasympathetic nervous system. This system controls specific body functions such as digestion, heart rate, and the immune system. These functions are involuntary, meaning you can't consciously control them.

Miscommunication in this system and with the heart and brain may cause a sudden drop in heart rate and blood pressure. This leads to fainting, often in reaction to a trigger such as food, temperature, or exercise. The doctor scheduled a tilt table test which showed that I had a problem indeed. A tilt table test is used to evaluate a possible cause of unexplained fainting. It can help determine if the cause is related to heart rate or blood pressure issues. You are strapped to a table that is elevated to a vertical position slowly, as a result, there is less blood flow to the brain and fainting can result. A second tilt table test was scheduled, and during that test, my heart stopped beating for a minute. With these results, I was scheduled to get a pacemaker and that changed my life for the better!

Since then, I have had three pacemakers implanted. Yes, I can still have fainting spells, but they have been few and far between since having the pacemakers. The real blessing is my heart won't stop if I faint because the pacemaker works to keep it beating. By the time I was diagnosed, I was in my early fifties. I had lived a good, rich life, but these spells had hung like a dark cloud over my head all those years. Finally, I was able to go off all the seizure medication I'd been on and regain control of my life.

God's goodness and mercy saw me through so much, and His presence never left me, nor will He ever leave you. I felt as though I had lived many years in "the valley of the shadow of death" as David spoke of in Psalm 23. God helped me see it for what it was all those years, just a shadow!

TRANQUILITY

Peace I leave with you. My peace I give to you; not as the world gives do I give to you. Let not your heart be troubled, neither let it be afraid.
John 14:27 NKJV

Once my blackout spells were treated and controlled, I had a new lease on life. The next few years were wonderful! My family and I were able to take trips to the Bahamas, Hawaii, and Italy, as well as travel throughout California, Oregon, and Arizona. We loved to take trips to northern Arizona. I could fish, hike and enjoy the outdoors once again! Living life without limitations was new to me. My spirit was energized and strengthened by traveling and enjoying the wonderment of God's world. It was during these years that I spent more time in the Word, and drew closer to Jesus, the Father, and Holy Spirit. God used me in many ways during this time to pray for people, to teach, to evangelize, and to do community outreaches, and deliverances.

I was involved in a nursing home outreach that touched my heart for the lonely and hurting. I quickly realized God had placed me there because He saw a need and He knew I could fill it. In addition to the outreach, I started going to the home to just visit, read the word of God, and pray over these sweet people. I had faithful people who had the same heart for this ministry helping me. We took the nursing home residents' prayer requests, prayed over them, and saw how eager they were for us to return to visit. We were the hands and feet of Jesus to them and were more blessed than the residents of the nursing home. Then covid-19 hit and the visits had to stop. This pained us greatly and we knew it also hurt the residents who had become our friends. Hopefully one day we can go back to this ministry as it is an important one. Just as

Ecclesiastes 3:1 says, "There is a time for everything and a season for every activity under the heavens."

This was a time of preparation for me, for what was coming in the next few years was no surprise to the Lord. He has been faithful all my life and continues to be so. He has always had a plan for me. He has one for you too! Jeremiah 29:11 says "For I know the plans I have for you, declares the Lord, plans to prosper you, plans to give you a hope and a future."

EXPRESSIONS OF HIS LOVE

I have loved you with an everlasting love, I have drawn you with unfailing kindness.
Jeremiah 31:3 NIV

I spent the next few years intently seeking the Lord. I found myself going wherever the Spirit was moving, and His presence was evident. This was in addition to attending regular church. I just couldn't get enough of Him! I would fast, pray, and let Him lead me. During this time, I met a lady at a conference that the Holy Spirit drew me to attend. We had lunch and decided we would meet to do street ministry in downtown Mesa, Arizona. What an experience! We prayed and asked God to bring people across our path that needed a touch from Him. We got our prayers answered in amazing ways. We started walking with some Bibles and tracts and set out on this adventure. Sure enough, God put the people He wanted us to encounter in our path at a bus stop. With the Holy

Spirit as our guide, we were able to pray with, minister to, and prophecy over the four people waiting for that bus. They would never be the same, and we wouldn't either. As we continued, we met two young men out on parole who were living at a local halfway house. They were out looking for employment, so we prayed with them for the perfect jobs. We also prayed for rededication to Jesus for one of the fellows, salvation for the other, and deliverance from tobacco, drugs, and alcohol for both. Then we prayed for the knee of the newly born-again young man. He had injured it in high school years before and just lived with the pain. God healed his knee that very day and we all rejoiced!

God was so very good to me at this time and showed me His love in so many ways. One conference I attended was so filled with praise and worship of His presence that miracles were happening all around. During one worship session, I looked at my hands. They had flecks of gold dust on them that had formed as I had worshipped! At another conference, oil appeared on the back of my left hand, again, when I was worshipping Him in all His Glory. I wasn't chasing after these manifestations. The signs appeared to me, and I believe they were meant to encourage me that He is a good, good God. He still uses signs and wonders to bless His people. Psalm 115:3 says "Our God is in heaven; He does whatever pleases Him." If He wants to send gold flakes, oil, or whatever sign of His glory so be it, He alone is God!

CONFRONTING EVIL

Behold, I give unto you the authority to trample on serpents and scorpions, and over all the power of the enemy, and nothing shall by any means hurt you.
Luke 10:19 KJV

A few years ago, my friend, Delia, and I joined together in prayer and fasting to help some people who reached out to us. These people had been experiencing some very difficult times. Months earlier the husband of the friend, who contacted us, had committed suicide. Since the suicide, the lady's daughter, son-in-law, and grandsons had moved in with her. After they moved in, some very strange things started happening. It was as though the house had become haunted. Strange apparitions of an old man began appearing in the kitchen, and eerie noises became common. Lights were randomly turned off and on, doors slamming by themselves, a piano downstairs playing late at night, and everyone stumbling and tripping down the stairs from the second floor. To my friend and me, it seemed something demonic was causing the problems. These eerie occurrences started tormenting the family after the suicide happened. This was a Christian family so we felt strongly about going to pray with them. That was our sole intent. Boy, were we in for a surprise! After fasting and praying all day, we went one evening after work to pray with the family. Delia asked me to do the talking while she remained in the background praying in the spirit. Once we arrived and the door opened, we knew something odd was going on. The entire family was dressed in winter coats, hats, and scarves. The two little grandsons, ages two and four, even had mittens on! It was a cool, rainy night in late November in Arizona, but certainly not cold enough for winter apparel.

The temperature was so cold in the entire house that it was frightening. Repairmen had been called out to check the furnace and thermostat. Everything worked fine until they left and then the temperature plummeted inside the house again! Brrrrrrrrrr!!

We all gathered in the living room. We prayed, anointed, and plead the blood of Jesus over everyone. Then we anointed each room in the home, binding the evil spirits, and commanding them to leave. A couple of the rooms particularly stood out as having a lot of activity from a demonic spirit. The Holy Spirit was with my friend and me in authority and we saw results. We felt the presence of evil and heavy oppression in the room where the suicide was committed. The oppression and heaviness left as we prayed and warred in the spirit. In another room, there was a trophy case full of samurai statues and swords. The statues appeared to look at us as we entered the room; we knew there was evil attached to them. We prayed in the Holy Spirit and spoke the word to bind and cast out these evil spirits from holding this family captive. We advised the family to dispose of the statues and swords – get them out of the house! (After we left, they did this.) While going through the rooms, anointing, and praying, the temperature became normal throughout the entire house! As we prayed one last time in the room with the statues, a ceiling light with a fan turned on above us and got brighter, then dimmed again as the fan went full speed! I commanded in the name of Jesus for that spirit to go, and immediately, the light went out and the fan stopped!

The family was grateful for our help and thanked us, saying they could now sleep peacefully once again. The little ones were especially grateful, as a demon had been manifesting and scaring them so they couldn't sleep at night. We felt great peace as we left, instructing them to *walk in their authority* as Christians if anything tried to come back. A few weeks later I received a call from the widow; I was expecting to hear how they were free of the demonic oppression – but instead, she reported the evil had returned! I told her to do what she had seen me and my friend do: bind those demons per Mathew 16:19, cast them out, and release God's spirit into that home! She called back a few weeks later and said nothing had changed. She decided they were just going to stay at the house and deal with the demonic oppression and strange occurrences. How sad I thought. We need to not only *know our authority* as Christians, but to *walk in it*, as Jesus said in Luke 10:19, "Behold, I have given you authority to tread on serpents and scorpions, and over all the power of the enemy, and nothing shall hurt you." I realized through this experience that we have a choice to walk with the Holy Spirit in His authority or not. The choice is up to us. My friend and I were not experienced in this type of ministry at the time, but God covered us, guided us, and kept us safe as we ministered. Our faith grew as we stepped out and trusted Him. He was guiding us as we were called to go to other homes to bind a demonic presence and release God's power and peace. God is faithful if you depend on Him!

If your prayer is sincere when you say, "Use me, Lord," be prepared to be used. Know that God is faithful to those he calls on and to those who call on Him, always! Jeremiah 33:3 says "Call unto me, and I will answer you, and show you great and mighty things which you did not know."

SUFFERING

Not only that, but we rejoice in our sufferings, knowing that suffering produces endurance, and endurance produces character, and character produces hope.
Romans 5:3-4 ESV

In November 2019, I went to the doctor for what seemed to be an ordinary, bothersome hemorrhoid. After some concern, I was sent to a colorectal doctor for a colonoscopy and biopsy. In December 2019 I learned it was not a hemorrhoid, but fast-growing, aggressive, squamous cell carcinoma—the big C! It was inoperable, so I would need chemotherapy and radiation. I showed up for my first round of chemotherapy, only to be told I was running a fever and needed to go to the hospital, where I was admitted for an infection. I was released three days later, tired and weak. On Christmas Eve I was scheduled to have a chemo port placed inside my chest and then thirty rounds of radiation and chemotherapy would begin.

Not exactly the Christmas gift I was wishing for, but God had me, this was all I needed to know during a season that should have been marked with joy and celebration. My treatments lasted into March 2020. I was in so much pain and agony from the radiation, I ended up in bed for several months trying to adjust to my new cancer-free body wracked with pain. Mentally I was ready to start living life again, knowing I was healed from cancer by God and the medical doctors he placed around me to treat it. Unfortunately, after ending my treatment, I spiked a high fever and went to the hospital for five days, during which I suffered from uncontrollable diarrhea due to the radiation. All this just exasperated the delicate condition of my skin, bowel, and everything else "down there." After resting for two months to regain strength and bowel control, things worsened. Blisters had formed inside my bowel and on the outside of my skin. It was the worst pain

I'd ever experienced. I couldn't sit, stand, lie, or barely ride in a car to my appointments…Something had to be done! I found peace in Him, sometimes moment to moment during this time. It was by far one of the most difficult times in my life. Some days I wanted to just quit, but I dug into the word, prayed, worshipped, and sought the Lord as never before!

At the end of July 2020, my doctor performed a temporary colostomy. The colostomy would circumvent the duress and irritation the radiation caused in my bowel. The first month of the colostomy was horrible. My skin was raw from irritation due to the colostomy bag continually leaking. My home health care nurse was invaluable during this time and assisted me as much as she could. My doctor decided I needed a different piece of equipment for the bag, which almost instantly solved the problem. My raw, wounded skin healed. My temporary colostomy eventually became permanent. This caused me to make many adjustments adapting to life with it, but God has seen me through it all. He is so very faithful. But God! As Psalm 73:26 says, "My flesh and my heart may fail; *But* God is the strength and my portion forever." I look back and often reflect on this time of suffering and forced stillness. I feel the strength that it brought about in me to overcome and focus on Him alone. I drew so close to God and cried out to Jesus so often for His peace, and He was so very gracious to grant me exactly what I asked for. I was having one of my last radiation treatments; I was in tears from the pain of it and just wanted it to be over. I asked Jesus to give me His peace. I shut my eyes. I had a vision of Him standing at my head, hands on my shoulders and He was telling me, "I have been here with you for *every* treatment." How that comforted me. It reassured me of His love and care for me. I had many caring and compassionate friends who helped me and my husband during this time. They brought us food, cleaned for us, sent me lovely cards, took me to treatments, and doctor appointments, and prayed for us both. My husband was such a steadfast helpmate in all of this, I don't know what I'd have done without him! All this gave me even deeper compassion for everyone I saw who was suffering, including those who came in for chemo and radiation treatments by themselves, (as they had no one to care for them). Those who were wheeled in by loved ones because they were too weak to walk, and many who were so much worse off than me. Suffering can be a very humbling experience if you allow it to be, and I know for me, it gave me Christ's compassion for others at a depth I'd never experienced before. I am still dealing with some effects of the radiation I received. I have had additional surgeries and procedures to deal with the chronic inflammation that was left behind as a result of the treatments that destroyed the cancer. While the doctors tell me I am in remission, I say I am healed! Thank you, Jesus! As 1 Peter 2:24 says, "…by whose stripes you **were** healed."

Throughout my life, I have lived with mysterious fainting spells, been diagnosed with a heart problem, and battled cancer. Each illness in my life was challenging, and stressful and created fear. 1 John 4:18 says, "There is no fear in love, but perfect love casts out fear because fear involves torment. But he who fears has not been made perfect in love." I now understand that if I walk in His love as He has shown me throughout my life, it forces any fear I have OUT! Having cancer solidified my peace in Him as I had never before experienced. I knew deep inside of my being His love in such an overwhelming way, that any fear melted away. I understand why Paul could say "For me to live is Christ, and to die is gain." Philippians 1:21. Through it all, Jesus has been walking right alongside me, holding my hand, as He tells me in Isaiah 41:10, "Fear not, for I am with you; Be not dismayed, for I *am* your God. I will strengthen you, yes, I will help you, I will uphold you with My righteous right hand." God has delivered me from the many floors I have found myself on. He has guided me through highs and lows every time I've cried out and called on Him, He's there! Once God and the doctors healed my body, I could see a piece of His plan for me which included: street ministry, nursing home ministry, teaching, deliverance, healing ministry, and becoming an author to spread His word. I can't help but serve such a loving, merciful God, whom I pray you also know, love, and serve. **GOD is GREAT! GOD is GOOD!**

LESSONS LEARNED

Give instruction to a wise man, and he will be still wiser; teach a righteous man, and he will increase in learning.
Proverbs 9:9 ESV

Oh, to be wise like David or Solomon! Throughout my life, God has guided me, protected me, sent me, watched over me, and instructed me. Have I always listened? No, unfortunately! I have to admit that despite God's guidance, at times, I have denied and dismissed it in my own life. But thank heavens, His mercy is new every day; His loving kindness and tender mercies crown me. "Herein is our love made perfect, that we may have boldness in the day of judgment: because as he is, so are we in this world." 1 John 4:17. I declare I am like Him in this world! And He never gives up on me!

NEVER!

I have learned:

- **To wait upon the Lord**, just as it says in Isaiah 40:31, the *life scripture* He gave to me so many, many years ago, "Those that wait upon the Lord shall renew their strength. They shall mount up with wings like eagles, they shall run and not be weary, they shall walk and not faint."

- **To not doubt but walk in faith** stated in Mark 11:23, "For assuredly, I say to you, whoever says to this mountain, "Be removed and be cast into the sea, and does not doubt in his heart, but believes that those things he says will be done, he will have whatever he says."

- **To not fear**, as per Isaiah 43:1, "Don't fear, for I have redeemed you; I have called you by name; you are Mine."

- **To walk in love**, just as Ephesians 5:1 says, "Therefore be imitators of God as dear children. And walk in love, as Christ also has loved us and given Himself for us, an offering and a sacrifice to God for a sweet-smelling aroma."

- **To be bold**, per Deuteronomy 31:6, "Be strong and of good courage, do not fear nor be afraid of them; for the LORD your God, He is the One who goes with you. He will not leave you nor forsake you."

- **To walk in His authority**, stated in Mathew 18:18-19, "Whatsoever you bind on earth shall be bound in heaven: and whatsoever you shall loose on earth shall be loosed in heaven...." Speak His Word to establish His kingdom here on earth. Speak His word to walk in His power.

- **To decree and declare** as priests and kings, stated in verses 1 Peter 1:9, Ephesians 1:20, and Mathew 16:19. These verses say to offer up to heaven God's word as a priest and to proclaim the word as a king downward to the earth, to walk as His ambassador on this earth. Ephesians 2:6 says "And raised us with Him and seated us with Him in the heavenly places in Christ Jesus."

- **To heal the sick**, as instructed in Mark 16:17-18, "And these signs will accompany those who believe: in my name, they will cast out demons; they will speak in new tongues; they will pick up serpents with their hands; and if they drink any deadly poison, it will not hurt them; they will lay their hands on the sick, and they will recover."

- **To forgive**, according to Mark 11:25, "And when you stand praying if you hold anything against anyone, forgive them, so that your Father in heaven may forgive you your sins."

- **To seek His wisdom**, just as James 1:5 tells us, that if you ask for wisdom, God will give it generously without finding fault.

- **To daily seek Holy Spirit** to fill me anew and afresh, and to be obedient to His voice. Mathew 7:7 says, "Ask, and it will be given to you; seek, and you will find; knock, and it will be opened to you." For everyone who asks receives, and he who seeks finds, and to him who knocks it will be opened." Acts 5:32 says that God freely gives the Holy Spirit to those who hear and obey Him.

- **And lastly, to make Micah 6:8 the standard to live by.** "He has told you, O man, what is good; and what does the Lord require of you but to do justice, and to love kindness, and to walk humbly with your God?"

- Make it a daily choice to **INTENTIONALLY** seek, go after, obey, and do what He tells you!

CHOOSING HIM

For if we live, we live to the Lord; and if we die, we die to the Lord. So, whether we live or die, we belong to the Lord.
Romans 14:8-9 NIV

I can't imagine my life without Jesus. What He has shown me, what He has brought me through, what He has imparted to me, the love that He continues to pour out to me, the forgiveness He extends to me, the peace that only He can give me …. Where would I be without Him? I would still be living a life of sin and remorse, regrets, and grief. Would you like to know the Jesus I know?

Salvation Prayer
Just say this simple prayer and He will be there immediately in your heart!

I come to You Father from the depths of my heart. I know I have sinned. I repent of my sins and confess with my mouth that Jesus Christ is the Son of God and died on the cross for me and took my sins. I believe He was raised from the dead. Lord Jesus, come into my heart and live in me now. I receive your Holy Spirit as my Comforter to help me obey You and do Your will. It's in Jesus' name that I believe and receive the things sincerely prayed for on this day.

Amen.

(Hebrews 11:6, 2 Corinthians 4:6, 5:21, John 1:1-3, 3:16)

If you said this prayer, rejoice! Jesus has now come into your heart to live ..... The adventure has only begun! Hallelujah!

Made in the USA
Las Vegas, NV
03 December 2023